# MOLDOVA

# MOLDOVA

THEN & NOW

Prepared by
**Geography Department**

**Lerner Publications Company**
Minneapolis

Series editors: Mary M. Rodgers, Tom Streissguth,
  Colleen Sexton
Photo researcher: Bill Kauffmann
Designer: Zachary Marell

Our thanks to the following for their help in preparing and
checking the text of this book: Dr. Craig ZumBrunnen,
Department of Geography, University of Washington; Keith
Eliot Greenberg; and Professor Paul Teoderescu.

### Pronunciation Guide

| | |
|---|---|
| Dniester | DNEE-ster |
| Gagauz | ga-GOWZ |
| Mircea | meer-CHAY-a |
| Snegur | snee-GOOR |
| Nicolae | nee-ko-LY |
| Ceausescu | chow-SHES-kew |
| *voivode* | VOY-voad |

Terms in **bold** appear in a glossary that starts on page 52.

LIBRARY OF CONGRESS CATALOGING-IN-PUBLICATION DATA

Moldova/prepared by Geography Department, Lerner Publica-
tions Company.
    p.    cm.—(Then & now)
  Includes index.
  Summary: Discusses the history, geography, ethnic mixture,
politics, economy, and future of the former Soviet Republic of
Moldova.
  ISBN 0-8225-2809-6 (lib. bdg.)
  1. Moldova—Juvenile literature. [1. Moldova.] I. Lerner
Publications Company. Geography Dept. II. Series: Then & Now
(Minneapolis, Minn.)
DK509.23.M65 1992
947'.75—dc20                              92-13499
                                             CIP
                                              AC

Manufactured in the United States of America
1  2  3  4  5  6  98  97  96  95  94  93

# • CONTENTS •

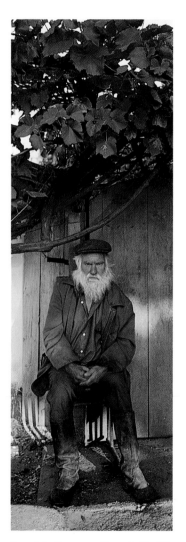

*An elderly man sits outside his house in Tiraspol, a city in southeastern Moldova.*

*"This is our home, our land, and we will fight for it."*

*Moldovan resident, 1990*

In 1992, the Soviet Union would have celebrated the 75th anniversary of the revolution of 1917. During that revolt, political activists called **Communists** overthrew the czar (ruler) and the government of the **Russian Empire.** The revolution of 1917 was the first step in establishing the 15-member **Union of Soviet Socialist Republics (USSR).**

The Soviet Union stretched from eastern Europe across northern Asia and contained nearly 300 million people. Within this vast nation, the Communist government guaranteed housing, education, health care, and lifetime employment. Communist leaders told farmers and factory workers that Soviet citizens owned all property in common. The new nation quickly **industrialized,** meaning it built many new factories and upgraded existing ones. It also modernized and enlarged its farms. In addition, the USSR created a huge, well-equipped military force that allowed it to become one of the most powerful nations in the world.

**Pastel-colored sculptures decorate a park in Kishinev, the capital of Moldova.**

In 1940, the Soviet Union took over **Bessarabia**, a province of the neighboring nation of Romania. Renamed the Moldavian Soviet Socialist Republic (SSR), this agricultural region along the USSR's southwestern border had an **ethnic Romanian** majority. Nevertheless, the Soviet leader Joseph Stalin ordered the building of new factories and brought in thousands of workers from the Soviet republics of Russia and Ukraine. Stalin also forced the inhabitants of **Soviet Moldavia** to replace their Latin alphabet with Cyrillic, the alphabet used in Russian and in some other Slavic languages.

The Moldavians never fully accepted Soviet occupation, and by the late 1980s a strong movement for independence was developing in the republic. A new political group, the Moldavian Popular Front, demanded self-rule and free elections. In the summer of 1990, the Moldavian parliament, against Soviet orders, officially changed the colors of the republic's flag to match the colors of Romania's flag. The legislature also renamed the country Moldova.

*In early 1991, before Moldova won its independence from the Soviet Union, special units of Soviet police put down this riot in Kishinev. Participants in the demonstration carried the three-color Moldovan flag.*

*The economy of Moldova is struggling to adapt to the collapse of the centrally planned system of the Soviet era. These citizens make extra cash by selling goods at an open market.*

*A building in Tiraspol flies the old flag of Soviet Moldavia. The city lies in the center of a narrow territory along the Dniester River that has a mostly Russian population. The region is seeking independence from Moldovan control.*

At the same time, the Soviet Union was in a period of rapid change and turmoil. The central government had mismanaged the economy, which was failing to provide goods. People throughout the vast nation were dissatisfied. The widespread movement for independence among the Soviet republics worried some old-style Communist leaders.

In August 1991, these conservative Communists used Soviet military power to try to overthrow the nation's president in a **coup d'état.** A demonstration against this action in the Moldovan capital of Kishinev (also spelled Chisinau) drew 100,000 protesters. The attempted coup failed within a few days and led to the breakup of the USSR. On August 27, Moldova declared its independence from the Soviet Union. Romania and other nations soon recognized Moldova as a free and self-governing country. In 1992, Moldova and several other former Soviet republics became new members of the **United Nations.**

# CHAPTER ONE

# The Land and People of Moldova

C overing 13,012 square miles (33,701 square kilometers), Moldova is a landlocked nation in southeastern Europe. One of the smallest republics in the former Soviet Union, Moldova is slightly larger than the state of Maryland and about equal in size to the Netherlands. Ukraine, another former Soviet republic, borders Moldova to the east, north, and south. To the west is Romania, a European state that shares a common language and culture with most of the Moldovan people. The Black Sea, which formed the southern coast of historic Bessarabia, now is separated from modern Moldova by territory belonging to Ukraine.

*Romanians make up the largest ethnic group in Moldova and generally belong to the Eastern Orthodox branch of Christianity. Here, churchgoers in Kishinev arrange food on tables outside a 19th-century Eastern Orthodox church.*

### • *Topography and Climate* •

Three river valleys running northwest to south-east contain most of Moldova's towns and population. In the west, the Prut River divides Moldova from Romania. To the east, the Dniester River forms part of Moldova's border with Ukraine. The Reut, a short tributary of the Dniester, flows within a narrow valley in central Moldova.

Deciduous (leaf-shedding) trees, especially oak, dot the hills and river valleys of the Belcay Steppe, a gently rolling plain in northern Moldova. This plateau lies at about 300 feet (91 meters) above sea level, rising in the north to about 2,000 feet (609 m). In central Moldova, thick forests of oak, ash, and maple trees flourish in the Kodry Hills. Vineyards and fruit orchards are common in central Moldova and along the valley of the Dniester. In southern

*Moldova's fertile soil yields a wide variety of crops, including grapes, peppers, tomatoes, cabbages, and squash.*

*The Reut River flows through the countryside of central Moldova.*

**Schoolchildren hike in the heavily forested Kodry Hills, which stretch across central Moldova.**

Moldova, the lower elevations and level plains of the Budzak Steppe also allow intensive farming.

Moldova's temperate climate and fertile soil have benefited the nation's farmers. Although cold, dry winds sometimes blow from the open plains of Ukraine, warmer breezes from the Black Sea moderate Moldova's weather. In Kishinev, summer temperatures average 68° F (20° C). Winters, which last about three months, are short compared to those in the rest of the former Soviet Union. January temperatures in Kishinev average 26° F (–5° C). About 20 to 25 inches (51 to 63 centimeters) of rainfall occur each year, with the heaviest downpours taking place during the early summer.

# MOLDOVA

Elevation

| 500 | 200 | 100 | 0 | Meters |
| 1640 | 656 | 328 | 0 | Feet |

| 0 | 40 | 80 | Kilometers |
| 0 | 25 | 50 | Miles |

BELCAY

Moldova R.

ROMANIA

*A Moldovan worker holds giant tobacco leaves that flourish in the warm climate of the Kodry region.*

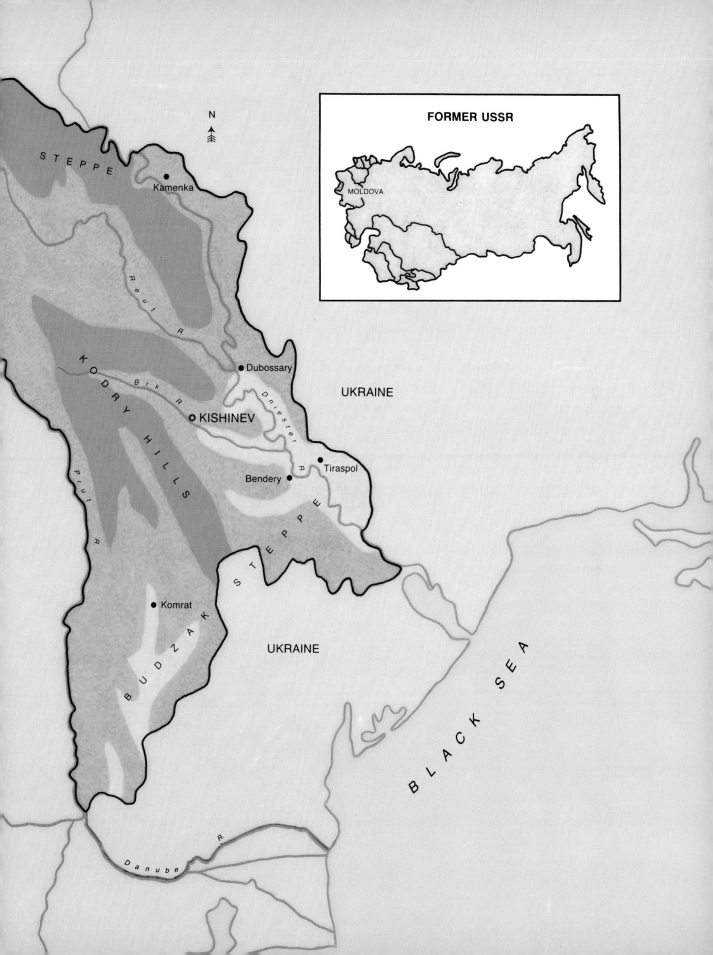

### • Cities •

Although Moldova has a high population density, the country has few large towns. Kishinev, the Moldovan capital and largest city, is home to 676,000 people. Founded in 1420, Kishinev lies on the Bik River in the center of Moldova. The city grew rapidly from a small village into an important rail junction between Romania and Russia during the 19th century. Kishinev suffered greatly during World War II (1939–1945), when bombing and street fighting destroyed more than 70 percent of the city's buildings.

After the war, engineers widened important thoroughfares, built tall office buildings, and planned industrial parks. Factories operating in the city's suburbs now account for nearly half of all industrial production in Moldova. The cultural capital of Moldova, Kishinev has a university, a science academy, and a music conservatory. The city also boasts museums, theaters, and the Moldovan Opera House. A series of parks and lakes offers residents open spaces and recreation.

Other large cities in Moldova include Tiraspol (population 182,000) and Bendery (population 130,000) on the Dniester River. The industrial town of Dubossary, on the eastern bank of the Dniester, has been a center of immigration from Russia and Ukraine since 1940. Beltsy (population 159,000), on the Reut River, is the largest city of northern Moldova.

*A flower seller in Kishinev puts together a bouquet of chrysanthemums.*

**Most of Kishinev's buildings date from the mid-20th century, when the city was rebuilt after being bombed during World War II (1939–1945). This modern square in the center of the capital has been the site of many independence demonstrations.**

**In June 1992, members of the Dniester Volunteer Corps drove a tank through the center of Bendery during street fighting between ethnic Russians and the Moldovan military.**

*Romanian customs and foods are common in Moldova. (Left) Wearing the national costume, a young Moldovan plays the cobza, a wooden, stringed instrument that accompanies folk songs and traditional dances. (Below) Baked goods and casseroles are favorite dishes among Moldovans.*

### • Ethnic Groups and Religion •

Moldova has long been a region of ethnic tension and conflict. After taking control of the territory in 1940, Soviet leaders insisted on calling the people Moldavians. The Soviets also suggested that Moldavians were closely related to Russians. But about two-thirds of the 4.4 million inhabitants of Moldova are ethnic Romanians who speak the Romanian language, a tongue based on ancient Latin.

**Ethnic Russians** within Moldova regard themselves as a separate republic, although the Moldovan government strongly opposes this position. Many of the 562,000 Russians and 600,000 **ethnic Ukrainians** who live in Moldova arrived after the Soviet annexation to seek factory jobs. Dubossary and Tiraspol are home to most of these workers and to new industries built under Soviet rule. Rus-

sians and Ukrainians make up about 27 percent of Moldova's population. Other Moldovan ethnic groups include Bulgarians, Belarussians, and **Gypsies.**

The 153,000 Turks, called **Gagauz**, live mainly around the southwestern city of Komrat. The Gagauz originated in central Asia and migrated to what was Bessarabia in the 18th and 19th centuries. Unlike most Turks, who are followers of the Islamic faith, the Gagauz practice the Christian religion. They proclaimed themselves independent after Moldova broke away from Soviet control and remain at odds with Moldova's Romanian majority.

Despite Soviet suppression of their faith, Moldova's 66,000 Jews have managed to retain their religious and cultural identity. Since 1989, about a dozen Jewish newspapers have been started, and Jewish religious leaders have opened a synagogue

(Above) *Seated on a wooden seahorse, a young Moldovan enjoys the summer sunshine.* (Below) *This student attends the University of Kishinev, which offers courses in physics, soil science, chemistry, biology, history, and language.*

*A Moldovan farmer holds a picture of his relatives, who originally came from neighboring Ukraine. Ethnic Ukrainians make up about 14 percent of Moldova's population.*

in Kishinev. Mircea Snegur, Moldova's president, has vowed to provide aid for developing Jewish education. Nevertheless, many Moldovan Jews emigrate to Israel each month.

Ethnic Romanians—as well as Russians and Ukrainians living in Moldova—belong to the Eastern Orthodox Church, a Christian sect that separated from the Roman Catholic Church in the 11th century. Under Soviet rule, Communist leaders strictly limited religious activities. The Soviet government

*The bride and groom hold candles during an Orthodox wedding ceremony in Kishinev. Moldova's ethnic Romanians, ethnic Russians, ethnic Ukrainians, and Gagauz follow the Eastern Orthodox faith.*

*Standing outside his Orthodox church, this deacon is a member of Moldova's Russian-speaking population.*

*Synagogues in Moldova, many of which were closed during the Soviet era, are again serving the country's small Jewish community. Here, a woman leaves the 200-year-old Beth Haknesset in Kishinev.*

ordered the destruction of Orthodox churches and sometimes punished clergy for leading services. Nevertheless, many Orthodox believers continued to practice their religion in secret.

The Soviet government eased restrictions on religion in the late 1980s. Since then, Orthodox Moldovans have repaired and restored many urban and rural churches. Although Moldovans now enjoy greater religious freedoms, there is still a shortage of priests to lead the congregations.

*Young seminarians (students training to be priests) relax at a newly opened monastery near the capital.*

*Education in Moldova includes many different studies and activities, ranging from adult education in English* (left) *to outdoor soccer games* (below).

## • *Education and Health* •

Under Soviet rule, ethnic Romanians had only limited access to higher education. Compared to the other Soviet republics, Moldavia had a low percentage of students attending secondary and postsecondary schools. This resulted from the Soviet Union's attempt to **Russify** Moldova. As part of this policy, Russian became the official language of education. Russian and Ukrainian students were given preference in university admissions, and the Soviet government passed laws to suppress Romanian culture within Soviet Moldavia. Nevertheless, Moldavians achieved nearly 100 percent literacy during the 20th century. More than 1,600 schools of all types now operate within Moldova.

After independence, the Moldovan government restored Romanian as the language of the schools. Moldovans have also built strong ties between the Romanian and Moldovan educational systems. Several thousand Moldovan students now attend schools in Romania. In addition, Moldovan teachers have replaced outdated Soviet textbooks with books donated to Moldova by the Romanian government.

More than 50 technical and vocational schools educate Moldovan students in trades and professional careers. Agricultural research institutes employ scholars and technicians. Nine universities, including the University of Kishinev, and other post-secondary schools also operate within Moldova.

One of the most respected institutions in Moldova—an important wine-producing country—is the College of Wine Culture. Located amid large vineyards, this 150-year-old school draws students from all over eastern Europe. Pupils begin courses at the college at age 15. About 300 wine experts graduate every year.

Although the Soviet government built new hospitals and clinics in Moldova, health standards suffered throughout the 1980s from a lack of modern equipment and facilities. These difficulties also plague the new Moldovan government, which now provides health care, mostly free of cost. Infant mortality—the number of babies who die within one year of birth—is 35 per 1,000 in Moldova. This rate is slightly lower than average among the former Soviet republics but is high by eastern European standards. Life expectancy in Moldova is 69 years—a figure that is roughly equal to the average life expectancy in the old USSR.

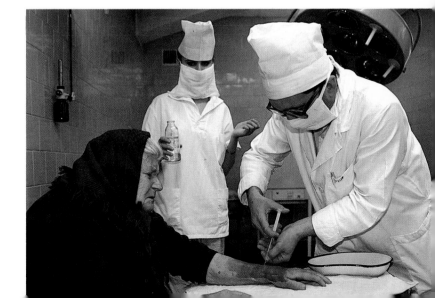

*A doctor gives his patient a painkiller in a Kishinev emergency clinic.*

# CHAPTER TWO

# Moldova's Story

Located along an important migration route from central Asia to eastern Europe, Moldova has suffered invasions from the west, the south, and the east. It did not become part of an organized state until the late 14th century. In more recent times, Moldova has been controlled by the Russian Empire, by Romania, and by the Soviet Union. Despite this turbulent history, the country's ethnic makeup has remained fairly stable. Although Russians, Ukrainians, Germans, Bulgarians, Jews, Turks, and Gypsies live in Moldova, the majority of its residents have always been Romanian.

## • Dacians and Romans •

One of the earliest peoples to establish communities in the area of Moldova were the Dacians. The ancestors of modern Romanians, the Dacians were farmers who organized themselves into

*In 1991, demonstrators thronged Kishinev's central square to support Moldova's decision to break free of Soviet rule.*

*A drawing shows ancient Dacians building fortified settlements in one of Moldova's mountain valleys. Although invasions drove the Dacians into the Carpathian Mountains, these old strongholds eventually became the foundation of small domains—called voivodates—that were ruled by local nobles.*

extended family groups. Around 2000 B.C., they began settling in the valleys and plains between the Dniester River and the Danube River, part of which forms Romania's southern border. By the 7th century B.C., the Dacians were trading with Greeks who had built commercial outposts on the coast of the Black Sea.

The Roman Empire, a powerful realm based on the Italian Peninsula to the south and west, conquered the Dacians in the 2nd century A.D. The invaders built roads, fortifications, and trading centers north of the Danube River and west of the Black Sea—an area the Romans knew as the province of Dacia. Many of Dacia's inhabitants learned Latin, the language spoken by Roman colonists.

A steady migration of peoples from the east and north forced the Romans to abandon Dacia in A.D.

271. Without Roman protection, the Dacians suffered waves of hostile invasions by Slavs from the north and Petchenegs from the plains north and east of the Black Sea. Many Dacians escaped into the Carpathian Mountains, a range that stretches across Transylvania (northeastern Romania).

*In the 1230s, the Tatar chief Batu Khan attacked many parts of southeastern Europe and destroyed the voivodates of Moldova.*

## • Settlement and Invasion •

Eventually, Slavic groups settled in southeastern Europe and intermarried with the Dacians. Missionaries converted many of the Dacians and Slavs to Christianity. In addition, the Romanian language developed from ancient Latin. New Slavic words made up a large part of the Romanian vocabulary.

For several centuries, no permanent states existed in the turbulent region north of the Danube River. To protect their lands, nobles known as **voivodes** established small realms—**voivodates**—on both sides of the Prut River. But the voivodes were unable to stop an invasion in the 13th century by the **Tatars.** A central Asian people, the Tatars had overrun much of Russia, which was then a principality (a state ruled by a prince).

Although they devastated farms and villages in the voivodates, the Tatars had withdrawn from the region by the early 1300s. According to legend, Bogdan, a voivode from Transylvania, then settled along the Moldova River in northeastern Romania. In the 1350s, Bogdan founded the principality of Moldavia, which included Bessarabia (modern Moldova). For more than a century, the young state prospered under strong leaders.

## • Rule of the Ottoman Turks •

The principality of Moldavia suffered a decline in the early 15th century, when rival factions in the government competed for control. At the same time, forces of the Ottoman Empire, based across the Black Sea in modern Turkey, were attacking southeastern Europe. Moldavia's leaders eventually were forced to submit to the demands of the Ottoman sultan (ruler), including heavy tribute (payment) in the form of crops and money.

Rather than put the area under direct rule, however, the sultan allowed Moldavia to remain a self-governing principality. The Turks appointed the Moldavian princes, but local landowners known as **boyars** maintained their independence. Many boyars acted as judges, administrators, and tax collectors.

In the late 15th century, the Moldavian prince Stephen the Great organized a force of peasants to resist the sultan. A religious crusader and a patron of the arts, Stephen had architects design new Orthodox churches throughout Moldavia. He also developed the principality's trade links with Europe and with the Middle East. Although the economy of Moldavia improved, Stephen was unable to gain allies for his struggle against Ottoman rule. After his death in 1504, the Moldavian princes again submitted to Turkish control.

Although it grew into a huge realm, the Ottoman Empire suffered from economic and political weakness. Tribute from its conquered states was not enough to support the sultan's court or the Turkish forces. In the 18th century, the empire began to lose territory in southeastern Europe. Seizing the opportunity to regain control of their land, the boyars of Moldavia asked for help from the Russian czar. In 1711, the Moldavian ruler Dimitri Cantemir signed the Treaty of Lutsk with the Russian czar Peter I (the Great). The treaty stated that Moldavia would be an independent state under the protection of the czar.

*A statue of Stephen the Great stands on a pedestal in a Kishinev park. During the late 1400s, Stephen governed the principality of Moldavia, which included present-day Moldova. Stephen's reign was marked by frequent conflict with armies from Ottoman Turkey. A respected and energetic leader, he raised a force of 55,000 peasants that defeated the Turks in several battles.*

Soon afterward, however, the Turks defeated the Russians in battle. Cantemir fled Moldavia to escape punishment by Ottoman forces. To keep the province under control, the Turks brought in Greek merchants to rule Moldavia and to collect tribute. These merchant-princes used the area mainly as a source of wealth, although many of them married into boyar families. The boyars kept their lands and laborers but lost most of their influence over local government.

**A Turkish miniature (small, detailed painting) shows Ottoman armies fighting in eastern Europe. Despite Stephen's victories, the Turks eventually overcame Moldova and controlled the region for more than 300 years.**

## • Border Conflicts •

During the 18th century, Moldavia fell into increasing turmoil. High taxes and frequent military actions on this Ottoman frontier caused poverty and famine. Bribery and corruption flourished among the Greek rulers, who sold administrative offices in Moldavia for their personal gain. Among Moldavia's attackers was the powerful Russian Empire, which occupied the principality in 1739 and 1769.

*In the late 19th and early 20th centuries, border disputes often changed the boundaries of Romania, Bulgaria, Hungary, and Moldova (then called Bessarabia). In the 1870s, Bessarabia was part of the Romanian state, but by 1918 Russia had annexed (taken over) the province.*

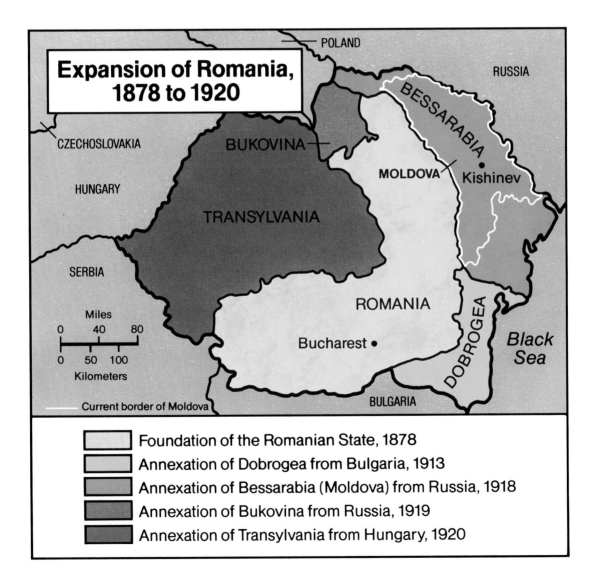

**Expansion of Romania, 1878 to 1920**

POLAND

RUSSIA

CZECHOSLOVAKIA

BUKOVINA

BESSARABIA

MOLDOVA • Kishinev

HUNGARY

TRANSYLVANIA

SERBIA

ROMANIA

Miles
0    40    80

0    50   100
Kilometers

Bucharest •

DOBROGEA

Black Sea

— Current border of Moldova

BULGARIA

|  | Foundation of the Romanian State, 1878 |
|---|---|
|  | Annexation of Dobrogea from Bulgaria, 1913 |
|  | Annexation of Bessarabia (Moldova) from Russia, 1918 |
|  | Annexation of Bukovina from Russia, 1919 |
|  | Annexation of Transylvania from Hungary, 1920 |

*In the early 1900s, many Jewish communities in Bessarabia suffered persecution. This Jewish family gathered in Kishinev to mourn the death of a relative killed in 1903.*

Ottoman control of Bessarabia lasted until 1812. In that year, the czar and the sultan signed the Treaty of Bucharest, which turned Bessarabia over to Russia. Conflict between Russia and the Ottoman Empire resumed when Russian forces marched into southeastern Europe in 1853. The Ottoman Empire then fought Russia in the Crimean War. In 1856, after Russia's defeat in this conflict, southern Bessarabia joined Romania. Within two decades, however, the Russians had invaded Bessarabia and by 1878 had regained control over the territory.

By the beginning of the 20th century, western Moldavia had become part of the newly united nation of Romania. Bessarabia (eastern Moldavia), however, remained under Russian control. Within a few years, Russia and the other large nations of Europe were preparing for military conflict. Russia joined Britain and France in an alliance against Germany. When Germany invaded France in the summer of 1914, World War I broke out in both western and eastern Europe.

## • The World Wars •

Russia suffered greatly during the war. Food shortages and military defeats caused widespread discontent within the empire. In 1917, Communist revolutionaries overthrew the Russian czar and government. After taking power, the Communists negotiated an end to the war with Germany. Romania, which had sided with Russia in World War I, seized Bessarabia after the conflict ended with Germany's defeat in 1918.

The Communist leaders of Russia founded the Union of Soviet Socialist Republics (USSR) in 1922. This state included Russia, Ukraine, and several other republics east of the Black Sea. Although it had become part of Romania, Bessarabia lay along the western border of the USSR and would soon be forced into another international war.

In 1939, the Soviet Union, ruled by Joseph Stalin, and Germany, ruled by Adolf Hitler, agreed to the **Molotov-Ribbentrop Pact.** This treaty banned hostilities between the two countries and allowed Stalin to **annex** lands in eastern Europe. In 1940, Stalin sent Soviet forces into Bessarabia to occupy the territory and to establish the Moldavian Soviet Socialist Republic.

### • *Soviet Rule* •

World War II began in the fall of 1939, when German forces swept through Poland. Britain, the Soviet Union, and later the United States became allies in the fight against Hitler. Germany's military victories, as well as political turmoil within Romania, prompted the Romanian government to side with

*A war memorial in the capital honors Soviet soldiers who died fighting the Germans in World War II. In 1940, just after the war began, the Soviet Red Army occupied Bessarabia and added it to the USSR as the Moldavian Soviet Socialist Republic. During the war, Soviet Moldavia was invaded and severely damaged by bombs. A treaty in 1947 legalized the Soviet Union's annexation of Bessarabia.*

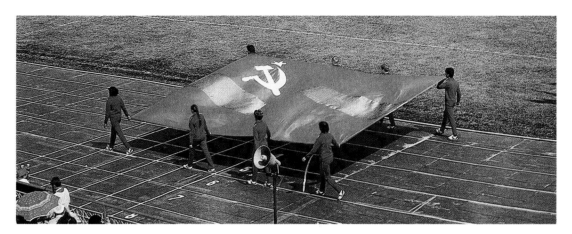

*At a sports event, athletes paraded the flag of Soviet Moldavia, which carried the yellow hammer and sickle—famous symbols of Soviet Communism.*

Hitler in 1940. Although Germany and the Soviet Union had agreed to avoid conflict, Hitler broke the Molotov-Ribbentrop Pact in 1941 by invading the Soviet Union. At the same time, Romanian forces attacked Soviet Moldavia and Ukraine.

The Soviet Union at first suffered great losses of territory, but the Soviet Red Army won decisive battles in 1942 and 1943. In the next year, the Red Army pushed the German forces back into eastern Europe and returned to Soviet Moldavia. After the Allies defeated Germany in 1945, Stalin sent loyal Communist officials into Soviet Moldavia to bring the republic firmly under his control. Under the terms of a treaty between Romania and the Allies signed in 1947, Bessarabia was formally turned over to the Soviet Union.

Although many of the Soviet Moldavians had relatives across the Prut River in Romania, Stalin announced that Moldavians and Romanians were now separate ethnic groups. He also denied that the people in the republic spoke Romanian, insisting instead that their language was Moldavian. The Soviets ordered the Moldavians to switch from the

Latin alphabet—which is used to write Romanian—to the Cyrillic alphabet, which Russians and Ukrainians use. In addition, the Soviets produced historical documents suggesting that the Moldavians had more in common with Russia than with Romania.

Many Moldavians who were unwilling to submit to Soviet rule took up arms. They were joined by Ukrainians who also sought independence. In 1950, Stalin placed Leonid Brezhnev, a Soviet official from Ukraine, in charge of putting down the Moldavian rebellion. Although Brezhnev was largely successful, Moldavians remained hostile to the Soviet government.

### • Russification •

In an attempt to Russify Soviet Moldavia, Stalin's government built new factories and homes in the republic and brought in new employees and residents. Russians and Ukrainians were encouraged—and sometimes forced—to move to Moldavian cities. The Soviets declared private farms to be Soviet property. The government-run **collective farms** were worked by families sent from all over the USSR.

The government also moved Moldavians to other parts of the Soviet Union. Immediately after the war, thousands were deported to central Asia and to Siberia, a remote region of Russia. After Stalin's death in 1953, the new Soviet leader Nikita Khrushchev ended the forced resettlements. Khrushchev, however, still offered financial bonuses to Moldavians who were willing to migrate to other areas.

Moldavia remained a small and quiet Soviet republic throughout the 1970s and 1980s. Brezhnev, who had helped to oust Khrushchev and then took power in 1964, continued the policy of Russification. The Soviet government closed Orthodox churches and Jewish synagogues. Russian became

*Under Soviet rule, Moldova's agricultural and industrial sectors changed. Small farms were forcibly combined into large estates, called collectives, that could raise huge amounts of crops, such as wheat (below). The Soviets also sent Russian and Ukrainian workers to Soviet Moldavia to operate the country's factories (bottom).*

the official language of education and of the media. Factories and collective farms in Soviet Moldavia were put under the direction of Russian and Ukrainian managers.

Under Brezhnev's leadership, the Soviet Union suffered a gradual economic breakdown. Since it gained most of its income from agriculture—rather than industry—Soviet Moldavia managed to escape the sharp decline in living standards that affected much of the industrialized USSR. Nevertheless, resistance to Russification and distrust of Moldavia's Communist leaders continued. In the late 1980s, the Soviet leader Mikhail Gorbachev introduced a new policy of **glasnost**—which means "openness" in Russian. Glasnost made it possible for Moldavian citizens to openly criticize Soviet rule.

### • *Independence and Ethnic Strife* •

In the late 1980s, many Moldavians were demanding an end to their republic's membership in the Soviet Union. Several anti-Soviet groups formed the Moldavian Popular Front in May 1989 and began organizing demonstrations in Kishinev. At one protest, Popular Front leaders called on Moldavia's leaders to replace Russian with Romanian as the country's official language. The gathering drew 500,000 people—more than 11 percent of the republic's population.

After several more rallies, the leaders of Soviet Moldavia agreed to some of the Popular Front's demands. Romanian again became the language of business, of education, and of radio and newspapers. Furthermore, Moldavians would again use the Latin alphabet and not Cyrillic. Street signs appeared in both Latin and Cyrillic, and Romanian names replaced the Russian names for major cities. Kishinev, for example, is known as Chisinau among

*A museum in Kishinev announces its hours of operation in Romanian* (left) *and Russian* (right). *In the 1950s, the Soviets introduced the Russian language, with its Cyrillic alphabet, to Soviet Moldavia. Even Romanian, which is written in the Latin alphabet, was transcribed into Russian lettering. In the late 1980s—after many demonstrations by the Popular Front—the Soviet government allowed Romanian again to become Soviet Moldavia's official language.*

ethnic Romanians, and the city of Bendery becomes Tighina in Romanian.

Ethnic Romanians celebrated these decisions, but Russian-speakers in the republic were strongly opposed. They marched through Kishinev, calling for the Soviet Union to overturn the new laws and to give the Russian and Romanian languages equal standing. In August 1989, 80,000 Russians walked off their jobs to protest what they saw as growing discrimination against them.

Tensions between ethnic Romanians and ethnic Russians worsened in the fall. At a parade in Kishinev in November, Popular Front members mounted tanks to stop an annual celebration of the Communist revolution of 1917. Three days later, Moldavians stormed and set fire to a government building. Soviet authorities quickly sent 2,000 troops to Kishinev, but the continuing unrest forced Semyon Grossu, Moldavia's Communist party leader, to step down.

Moldavians also supported an anti-Communist revolution in Romania by sending food and medical supplies across the Prut River. After the Romanian dictator Nicolae Ceausescu was overthrown and executed in December 1989, Moldavian relief workers crossed the border and were cheered by the Romanians as heroes. Despite the years of Soviet occupation, most Moldavians and Romanians regarded themselves as members of a single nation. In Kishinev and in the Romanian capital of Bucharest, crowds at street demonstrations called for the reunification of the western and eastern parts of historic Moldavia.

### • *Recent Events* •

Demonstrators occupied the headquarters of the Moldavian Communist party in June 1990 and turned the buildings over to local officials and charities. In the same month, members of the Moldavian parliament ignored Soviet orders and changed the republic's name to Moldova. They also adopted the blue, yellow, and red colors of Romania's flag for the Moldovan flag.

Meanwhile, Russians living along the Dniester River, as well as Gagauz in the city of Komrat, declared themselves to be separate republics.

**In 1989,** *members of the Popular Front gathered in Kishinev to voice their enthusiasm for independence.*

When the Soviet Union threatened to annex the industrial Dniester region, mobs of ethnic Romanians attacked their Russian and Gagauz neighbors.

In the summer of 1991, Gorbachev outlined a treaty that would allow the Soviet republics greater independence. Angered at what they viewed as Gorbachev's weakness, a group of Communist officials tried to seize control of the Soviet government in August. During this takeover bid—called a coup d'état—Soviet generals ordered Moldova's leaders to declare a state of emergency. Instead, the Moldovans went on television and radio to urge the people to protect Moldova. After 100,000 pro-independence Moldovans went into the streets to protest the coup, Soviet soldiers retreated.

Demonstrations in the USSR's largest cities thwarted the attempted coup. But the Communist party rapidly lost power, and Gorbachev could do little to stop the Soviet republics from leaving the union. On August 27, Moldova's parliament announced the country's independence. Three days later, Romania became the first nation to officially recognize the independent nation of Moldova.

### • An Uncertain Future •

By December 1991, the USSR was quickly falling apart. Ukraine and several other Soviet republics formed the **Commonwealth of Independent States.** In the spring of 1992, after joining the com-

*Near the city of Dubossary, which lies within a largely Russian-speaking region, a flower arrangement commemorates people who have died in Moldova's ethnic conflicts.*

*Moldova's parliament building now carries the national coat of arms adopted in late 1990. The emblem is also part of the country's flag, whose colors are the same as those on the flag of Romania. By August of 1991, Moldova had succeeded in leaving the USSR, and Romania was the first country to recognize the new nation.*

monwealth, Moldova gained a seat in the United Nations.

Despite their newly won independence, Moldovans have joined an economic alliance with the other members of the commonwealth. Some Moldovan politicians believe that Moldova is tied to these states through long-standing trade practices. The alliance may help Moldovan companies acquire raw materials and may also provide a market for finished goods.

Moldovans have formed several new political parties. The Popular Front is pushing for greater independence as well as the return of southern Bessarabia, which became part of Ukraine during the Soviet occupation. Former members of the banned Communist party, many of whom are ethnic Russians, still make up a powerful group within Moldova. Some of them want to restructure the Moldovan economy to permit private businesses and free markets. Other Russians wish to return to the strict methods used by the Soviet government before Gorbachev.

The Russian parties have worked closely with the Gagauz. Both groups oppose the control of Moldova's government by ethnic Romanians. The largest Gagauz organization is the **Gagauz Halky** (Gagauz People), which wants the southern and eastern parts of Moldova to become independent. Other organizations in the country represent a variety of interests. Women, farmers, and environmentalists, for example, each have their own political parties.

Although it has received international recognition as an independent state, Moldova still suffers violence among its various ethnic groups. Unless the country's leaders can agree to share political power, all the citizens of Moldova will face continuing civil strife.

# CHAPTER THREE

# Making a Living in Moldova

On the day that Moldova declared independence, the country's prime minister admitted that difficult times were ahead. The official was quick to add, however, that Moldova's plentiful fertile land gave the country a hopeful economic future. Moldova's farming **cooperatives**—employee-owned and operated ventures—have been successful. The country also benefits from the many factories that were built during the Soviet occupation but that are now Moldovan property.

Nevertheless, the years of Soviet rule in Moldova created an inefficient system of producing and marketing food and finished goods. Since the Soviet government set all production **quotas** and paid low prices for goods, workers were not motivated to work hard and to increase production. Goods that were hard to find at government shops were available on the **black market** only at expensive prices.

*Mounds of corn represent some of the output of a large collective farm in northern Moldova. Although collective farming failed in many other former Soviet republics, it fared better in Moldova. Instead of being split up into small farms, these huge estates may become cooperative farms, in which the workers operate the property as a profit-making venture.*

The collapse of the Soviet Union caused a rapid decline in the value of the ruble, the Soviet currency. As a result, factory managers in Moldova are unable to purchase raw materials with rubles and are forced to barter, or exchange, their goods for needed supplies. The Moldovan government may create a new currency that will be fixed to the value of the Romanian leu. This action would tie the economies of the two countries closer together.

Moldova's economy is dependent on trade with Ukraine and with other former Soviet republics. An extensive transportation network connects Moldova with eastern Europe by way of Romania. In addition, direct flights have been reestablished between Kishinev and Bucharest. These links will enable Moldovan companies to move their exports to foreign markets more easily.

(Above) *A shopper examines a blouse at a department store in Kishinev.* (Below) *In a suburb of the capital, an industrial area flies the flags of many European countries with which Moldova hopes to establish trade relations.*

In autumn, workers wrap the bark of apple trees with thick strips of cloth (left and right). The cloth protects the bark from being burned by the strong winter sun or eaten by deer and rabbits. A woman (below) carries a bucket of ripe tomatoes grown on a farm in southern Moldova.

## • *Agriculture* •

With rich soil and plentiful rainfall, Moldova enjoys ideal conditions for crop growing. More than half of the country's land is under cultivation. Collective farms in Soviet Moldavia exported fruit and vegetables to the rest of the USSR. In addition, Moldova produced one-quarter of all the wine made within the Soviet Union.

Farmers harvest sugar beets and grains, such as barley, wheat, and corn, in northern Moldova. Sunflowers flourish in this region's warm climate, providing both seeds and oil. Vineyards, fruit orchards, and tobacco fields exist in the valleys of the Kodry Hills in central Moldova. The orchards produce apples, plums, peaches, apricots, and walnuts. The fertile soils of the Kodry Hills, as well as the mild Moldovan climate, favor the raising of wine grapes, and wine is one of the republic's best-known exports.

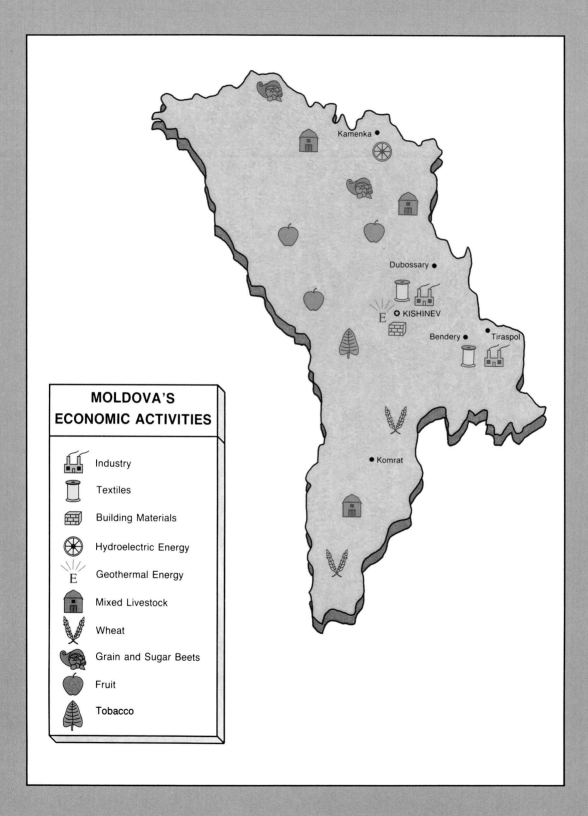

MOLDOVA'S
ECONOMIC ACTIVITIES

Industry

Textiles

Building Materials

Hydroelectric Energy

E Geothermal Energy

Mixed Livestock

Wheat

Grain and Sugar Beets

Fruit

**Tobacco**

Kamenka

Dubossary

E KISHINEV

Bendery • Tiraspol

• Komrat

(Above) **Horses haul freshly harvested hay from a field in southern Moldova.** (Below) **Wicker baskets hold the fruit of a vineyard in the Kodry Hills.**

In the valley of the Dniester in southern Moldova, cooperative farms grow tomatoes, eggplants, and peppers. Farmers raise cattle, pigs, goats, poultry, and sheep throughout the country. In southern Moldova, a drier climate favors wheat growing, as well as pasture for livestock.

While the government-run collective farms often failed to reach their quotas in other Soviet republics, the experiment had a measure of success in Moldova. Some Moldovan leaders believe that, rather than dividing the land and redistributing it to individual families, groups of workers should continue to farm the large estates that were formed under Soviet rule. These cooperatives would be furnished with modern machinery for planting and harvesting. Part of the funding for new equipment is expected to come from foreign investors.

### • Manufacturing and Energy •

A lack of mineral deposits has hampered the growth of Moldovan industry. In this agricultural country, food processing has remained the largest manufacturing business. Mills refine flour and sugar, and canneries process Moldova's abundant crops of vegetables and fruit. Wine and tobacco are other important products. A small textile industry has developed in Bendery. Factories in Kishinev make shoes, furniture, textiles, chemicals, food products, farm machinery, and building materials.

Many of Moldova's industries are located along the Dniester River, where the Soviets started factories that employed Russian and Ukrainian workers. These plants produce building materials, textiles, shoes, and finished metals. The conflict between ethnic Romanians and ethnic Russians in this region, however, has created an uncertain future for the cities and for the industries along the Dniester.

New power stations in Moldova generate electricity through the use of heated underground water. Engineers designed and built these **geothermal** plants in many of the country's larger towns. Most of Moldova's energy still comes from hydropower plants at Kamenka and Dubossary on the Dniester River.

Since the Dniester area supplies most of Moldova's consumer goods and electricity, residents of other parts of the country would have much to lose if political problems in the area worsen. In addition, Moldova must rely on oil imports from Russia and from other former Soviet republics. Closer ties with Romania may allow Moldova to import Romanian oil at favorable prices in the future.

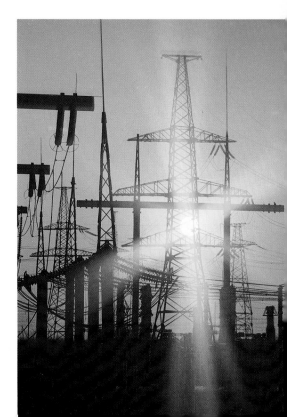

(Top) *Wine making is a successful business in Moldova. This worker operates a complex control panel that monitors the crushing and fermentation of grapes.* (Bottom) *Power lines bring electricity into Moldova from Bulgaria.*

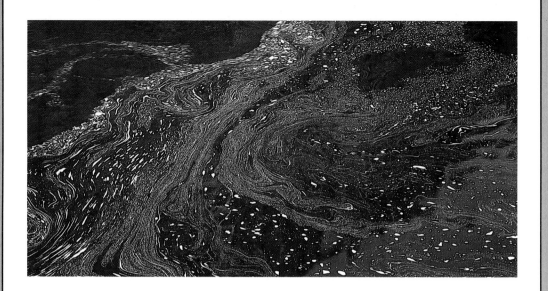

## DOWNSTREAM IN MOLDOVA

In 1983, a dam on a tributary of the Dniester River in Ukraine collapsed. Hazardous wastes from a fertilizer plant poured into the river, contaminating the waters that run downstream through Moldova to the Black Sea. The toxic wastes killed local fish and endangered Moldovans who depend on the Dniester for their water. This accident is just one example of Moldova's vulnerability to the environmental actions of neighboring nations.

Air pollution also threatens the health of many Moldovans. Officials in eastern Europe and in the old USSR did not install effective pollution controls in their industries. As a result, the emissions from smokestacks in Ukrainian and Romanian factories drifted over Moldova. Moldova also has contributed to the problem of air quality with its own unmonitored industries.

Under Soviet rule, Moldova accepted toxic wastes for landfills that did not meet international sanitary regulations. In addition, Soviet industries dumped wastes wherever they wanted, despite Soviet laws designed to prevent such activities.

In recent years, increasing numbers of Moldovans have voiced their concerns about environmental hazards in their country. With the help of citizens in neighboring nations, Moldovans are cleaning their air, their land, and their water resources.

# CHAPTER FOUR

# What's Next for Moldova?

Although no one is sure what Moldova's status will be in the years to come, the country's leaders have successfully set up democratic institutions. The Communist party no longer governs the area, and the remnants of Soviet power are disappearing. Soon after the Moldovan parliament declared independence, the republic's lawmakers passed resolutions demanding that all Soviet troops withdraw. Although Moldova's military is now responsible for the country's defense, Russian troops remain on Moldovan soil. They have fought beside Russian-speakers in Moldova who are seeking independence.

The Popular Front has sent forces to keep order in the Russian and the Gagauz areas. Many non-Romanians feel that these squads are brutalizing Moldova's minority ethnic groups. Violent clashes between Russians and Moldovans have claimed hundreds of lives. The Gagauz have called on their fellow Turks from around the world to aid them in their fight against Moldova's ethnic Romanians. Although there are only 153,000 Gagauz in

*Colorful laundry brightens a garden in Kishinev, where few people can afford washing machines or dryers. Moldova's efforts to expand its commercial ties to Europe may allow the country to import more consumer goods.*

Moldova, they have willingly engaged in street battles with their neighbors.

Many ethnic Romanians support joining Moldova with Romania. Despite the fact that Moldovans have adopted Romania's national colors and its national anthem, reunification may not be in Moldova's best interest. Under the rule of dictator Nicolae Ceausescu, the Romanian economy suffered more than that of Soviet Moldavia. Even Popular Front leaders say that joining Romania will mean a drop

*A young Moldovan waits in line to buy bread at a government-run store.*

## FAST FACTS ABOUT MOLDOVA

| | |
|---|---|
| Total Population | 4.4 million |
| Ethnic Mixture | 64 percent Moldovan<br>14 percent Ukrainian<br>13 percent Russian<br>3 percent Gagauz<br>2 percent Bulgarian |
| CAPITAL and Major Cities | KISHINEV, Tiraspol, Bendery, Dubossary |
| Major Languages | Romanian, Russian |
| Major Religion | Eastern Orthodox |
| Year of inclusion in USSR | 1940 |
| Status | Fully independent state; member of Commonwealth of Independent States; admitted to the United Nations in 1992; ethnic unrest among Gagauz, Russians, and Moldovans |

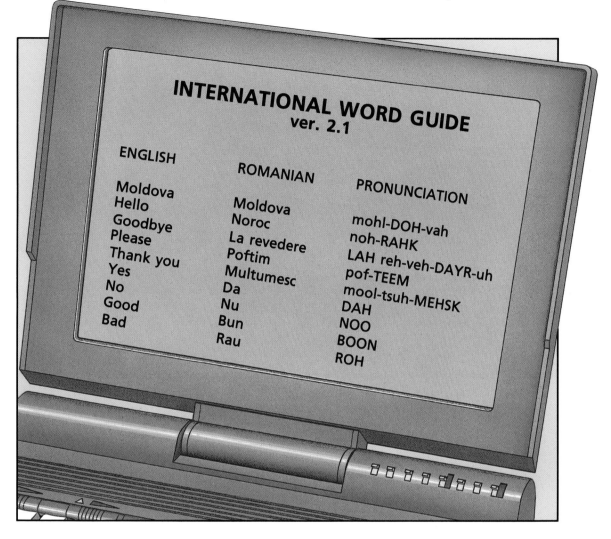

INTERNATIONAL WORD GUIDE
ver. 2.1

| ENGLISH | ROMANIAN | PRONUNCIATION |
|---|---|---|
| Moldova | Moldova | mohl-DOH-vah |
| Hello | Noroc | noh-RAHK |
| Goodbye | La revedere | LAH reh-veh-DAYR-uh |
| Please | Poftim | pof-TEEM |
| Thank you | Multumesc | mool-tsuh-MEHSK |
| Yes | Da | DAH |
| No | Nu | NOO |
| Good | Bun | BOON |
| Bad | Rau | ROH |

in Moldova's standard of living. Also, many people in Moldova feel that the Romanian government is still controlled by people who do not respect democracy.

Moldova may lose the power to make important economic and political decisions if it reunifies with Romania. Whether it joins its western neighbor or not, Moldova cannot survive as an isolated nation. It must settle its ethnic troubles, establish firm trade agreements with other former Soviet republics, and work toward cooperation among its competing political parties.

**annex:** to add a country or territory to the domain of another nation by force.

**Bessarabia:** a name for the land between the Prut and Dniester rivers in southeastern Europe. Bessarabia made up the easternmost territory of the principality of Moldavia. After the Soviet Union occupied Bessarabia in 1940, the region was brought into the Union of Soviet Socialist Republics as the Moldavian Soviet Socialist Republic.

**black market:** an informal system of exchanging goods that operates outside the state-owned distribution system.

**boyar:** one of the landowning nobles who administered Moldavia from the 15th to the 18th centuries.

**collective farm:** a large agricultural estate worked by a group. The workers usually received a portion of the farm's harvest as wages. On a Soviet collective farm, the central government owned the land, buildings, and machinery.

**Commonwealth of Independent States:** a union of 11 former Soviet republics that was created by the leaders of Russia, Belarus, and Ukraine in December 1991. The commonwealth, which includes Moldova, has no formal constitution and functions as a loose economic and military association.

**Communist:** a person who supports Communism—an economic system in which the government owns all farmland and the means of producing goods in factories.

*As a symbol of their rejection of the Soviet system, Kishinev's officials renamed this street. It once commemorated Vladimir Lenin, the founder of Soviet Communism, but now is called Stefan cel Mare (Stephen the Great) Boulevard.*

**cooperative:** a farm, factory, or other enterprise in which the members of a group produce and market goods and get a share of the profits.

**coup d'état:** French words meaning "blow to the state" that refer to a swift, sudden overthrow of a government.

**ethnic Romanian:** a person whose ethnic heritage is Slavic and who speaks Romanian.

**ethnic Russian:** a person whose ethnic heritage is Slavic and who speaks Russian.

**ethnic Ukrainian:** a person whose ethnic heritage is Slavic and who speaks Ukrainian.

**Gagauz:** a member of the Turkish ethnic group within Moldova that originated in central Asia.

**Gagauz Halky:** a political organization formed by the Gagauz people that demands independence for Gagauz areas in southern and eastern Moldova.

**geothermal:** a form of energy using heated underground water and steam to generate electricity.

***glasnost:*** a Russian word meaning "openness" that describes a Soviet policy of easing restrictions on writing and speech.

**Gypsies:** a nomadic people who live throughout Europe and who make up a small percentage of Moldova's population.

**industrialize:** to build and modernize factories for the purpose of manufacturing a wide variety of consumer goods and machinery.

**Molotov-Ribbentrop Pact:** a political agreement negotiated by Vyacheslav Molotov of the Soviet Union and Joachim von Ribbentrop of Germany. Signed in 1939, the agreement said that the two nations would not attack one another or interfere with one another's military and political activities.

*Under Soviet rule, this vehicle-assembly plant was required to produce a quota, or specified number, of tractors.*

**quota:** the government-set amount of factory goods or food that a group is told to produce.

**Russian Empire:** a large kingdom that covered present-day Russia as well as areas to the west and south. It existed from roughly the mid-1500s to 1917.

**Russify:** to make Russian by imposing the Russian language and culture on non-Russian peoples.

**Soviet Moldavia:** a republic of the USSR formed in the historic region of Bessarabia after 1945.

**Tatar:** a member of a Turkic ethnic group that originated in central Asia.

**Union of Soviet Socialist Republics (USSR):** a large nation in eastern Europe and northern Asia that consisted of 15 member-republics. It existed from 1922 to 1991.

**United Nations:** an international organization formed after World War II whose primary purpose is to promote world peace through discussion and cooperation.

***voivode:*** one of the landowning nobles who established small states, called ***voivodates,*** in Moldavia before the region was organized as a principality.

*Farm workers bring home armfuls of chickens that can be fattened and slaughtered or used to provide eggs.*

## • *Photo Acknowledgments* •

Photographs are used courtesy of: pp. 1, 6, 16, 18 (left and right), 19 (bottom left and bottom right), 20 (left and right), 21 (left), 22 (left and right), 23, 36, 39, 42 (top and bottom), 43 (top left and top right), 46 (top), 50 (right), 52, 55, Jeff Greenberg; pp. 2, 9 (right), 10, 38, 48, © Yury Tatarinov; pp. 5, 9 (left), © Caroline Penn; pp. 8, 12 (left), 13, 17 (bottom), 24, 32, 37, 45 (top and bottom), 46 (bottom), TASS / SOVFOTO; pp. 12 (right), 14, 19 (top), 33, 34, 35, 54, V. M. Sinitsky; p. 17 (top), M. Eugene Gilliom; p. 21 (right), © G. Pinkhassov / MAGNUM; p. 26, The Mansell Collection; pp. 27, 31, Independent Picture Service; p. 28, Romanian Cultural Center; p. 29, Cultural and Tourism Office of the Turkish Embassy; p. 40, © Bruno Barbey / MAGNUM; p. 43 (bottom), Sergej Schachowski; p. 47, VU / © Jon Bertsch. Maps and charts: pp. 14–15, 44, J. Michael Roy; pp. 30, 50, 51, Laura Westlund.

Covers: (Front) Jeff Greenberg; (Back) © Yury Tatarinov

| | | DATE DUE | |
|---|---|---|---|
| | | | |
| | | | |
| | | | |
| | | | |
| | | | |
| | | | |
| | | | |
| | | | |
| | | | |
| | | | |